NFL TODAY

THE STORY OF THE
CHICAGO BEARS

NFL TODAY

THE STORY OF THE CHICAGO BEARS

NATE LEBOUTILLIER

CREATIVE EDUCATION

Cover: Bears offense, 1963 (top), linebacker Brian
Urlacher (bottom)
Page 2: Linebacker Brian Urlacher
Pages 4–5: 2007 Chicago Bears
Pages 6–7: Kick returner Devin Hester

....

Published by Creative Education
P.O. Box 227, Mankato, Minnesota 56002
Creative Education is an imprint of
The Creative Company
www.thecreativecompany.us

Design and production by Blue Design
Design Associate: Sarah Yakawonis
Printed in the United States of America

Photographs by Alamy (David Ball), AP Images,
Getty Images (Lee Balterman/Sports Illustrated,
Vernon Biever/NFL, Scott Boehm, Jonathan Daniel,
James Drake/Sports Illustrated, Bill Eppridge//Time
& Life Pictures, Focus On Sport, Scott Halleran, Jed
Jacobsohn, Ali A. Jorge/NFL, Kidwiler Collection/
Diamond Images, Don Lansu/NFL, Streeter Lecka,
Al Messerschmidt, Al Messerschmidt/NFL, Donald
Miralle, Ronald C. Modra/Sports Imagery, Paul
Natkin/NFL, Pro Football Hall Of Fame, Pro Football
Hall Of Fame/NFL, Robert Riger, Paul Spinelli, Vic
Stein/NFL Photos, Herbert Weitman/NFL)

Library of Congress Cataloging-in-Publication Data

LeBoutillier, Nate.
The story of the Chicago Bears / by Nate
LeBoutillier.
p. cm. — (NFL today)
Includes index.
ISBN 978-1-58341-750-8
1. Chicago Bears (Football team)—History—Juvenile
literature. I. Title. II. Series.

GV956.C5L43 2009
796.323'640977311—dc22   2008020707

First Edition
9 8 7 6 5 4 3 2 1

CONTENTS

ON THE SIDELINES

MEET THE BEARS

PAPA BEAR
STARTS A FAMILY

X Chicago has earned fame for many things over the years, including its rich history in the railroad and meat packing industries, its ornate skyscrapers, and its passionate sports fans.

Located on the southern tip of the third-largest of the Great Lakes, Lake Michigan, the city of Chicago was founded in the 1830s as a small grain and livestock trading post. Since that time, Chicago has grown into the largest city in the midwestern United States. With almost three million people, it is today the third-largest city in America behind New York and Los Angeles. Its 110-story Willis Tower is the tallest building in America, and the city experiences strong winds that blow in off the lake and howl between the big skyscrapers.

The people of Chicago are also big on professional sports. And no team has enjoyed more success in the "Windy City" than the town's National Football League (NFL) franchise. After settling in Chicago in 1921 and being named the Bears—a name intended to tie in with the city's beloved Cubs baseball team—the club quickly made its growl heard across the NFL.

The story of the Chicago Bears begins with one man: George Halas. In 1920, when he was a 25-year-old athlete and businessman, Halas helped found a pro football team called

the Staleys in the nearby town of Decatur. A year later, he moved the club to Chicago and soon renamed it the Bears. Halas, who would become known as "Papa Bear," would own the Chicago Bears for the next 62 years, also acting as coach for 40 of them.

Halas did a little bit of everything in the team's early years. He sold tickets, taped ankles, shoveled snow, coached, and put himself into games as an offensive and defensive end. He was also a football innovator and the first coach to schedule daily practices and study game films. Thanks to his efforts and those of such players as running back Ed "Dutch" Sternaman (a part-owner of the team), Chicago was an instant success, going 9–1–1 in 1921 and winning the league championship.

Halas ensured that the Bears would remain a powerhouse for some time by signing two exceptional running backs in the years that followed. The first was Red Grange, who joined the team as a rookie in 1925. In college, Grange had once run for 263 yards and 4 touchdowns in a single quarter, and his shifty running style earned him the nickname "The Galloping Ghost." Grange was the featured attraction as the Bears went on a famous 19-game cross-country tour in 66 days in 1925 and 1926.

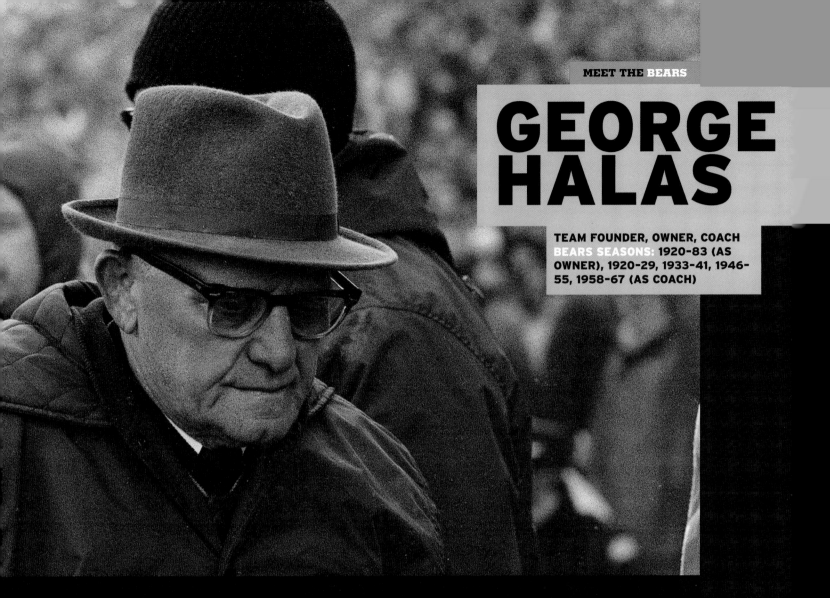

GEORGE HALAS

TEAM FOUNDER, OWNER, COACH
BEARS SEASONS: 1920-83 (AS OWNER), 1920-29, 1933-41, 1946-55, 1958-67 (AS COACH)

Born and raised on the west side of Chicago, George "Papa Bear" Halas founded, played for, coached, and owned the Chicago Bears football team. While studying at the University of Illinois, Halas played football, basketball, and baseball. He spent time in the U.S. Navy and played 12 games for the New York Yankees baseball team as an outfielder, then he switched over to football. He founded a team called the Decatur Staleys in 1920 that would become the Chicago Bears by 1922. Halas played for the Staleys/Bears from 1920 to 1929, mostly on defense, and once returned a fumble 98 yards for a touchdown. In the 1930s, he concentrated solely on coaching, building the Bears into a powerhouse that won NFL championships in 1932, 1933, 1940, 1941, 1943, 1946, and 1963. His players described him as a taskmaster, and he was the first coach to hold daily practice sessions and analyze films of games to further his coaching strategies. Among his accomplishments was the perfecting of the T-formation (an offensive set in which three running backs lined up five yards behind the quarterback), which became all the rage in football.

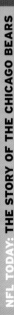

ON THE SIDELINES

SOLDIER FIELD

For the first 49 years of their existence, the Chicago Bears made their home at Wrigley Field. Then, in 1971, when the NFL ruled that all teams must play in stadiums with room for at least 50,000 fans, the Bears moved across town and into Soldier Field. Located only a few hundred yards west of Lake Michigan, Soldier Field had been constructed in the early 1920s as a memorial to American soldiers who had died in wars. Built to resemble great buildings of ancient Greece and Rome, Soldier Field was a versatile recreational venue that hosted championship boxing matches, rodeos, car races, circuses, and operas, among other events. In 2002 and 2003, the grand old stadium was essentially rebuilt at a cost of almost $630 million. Soldier Field's most identifiable features—its classical, 100-foot colonnades—were preserved, but they were dwarfed by a new metallic façade that raised the seating structure much higher. Although it seemed a majority of fans disliked the new, futuristic-looking exterior (many people said it looked like a flying saucer had landed on the stadium), most agreed that Soldier Field's interior was improved, offering better viewing angles.

Grange was joined in the Bears backfield in 1930 by fullback Bronislau Nagurski, better known as "Bronko." At 6-foot-2 and 230 pounds (a size considered enormous in those days), the northern Minnesota farmboy was a punishing runner and a remarkably skilled passer, but he was perhaps most fearsome as a blocker who paved the way for Grange. "When you hit him, it was like getting an electric shock," said Grange. "If you hit him above the ankles, you were likely to get yourself killed."

The Bears won two NFL championships in the 1930s. Chicago featured a number of great players during those years, including speedy running back Beattie Feathers and rough-and-tumble center George Trafton. But Grange and Nagurski were the heart of the team. The Bears won the 1932 championship when the NFL held its first-ever playoff game. The conditions were cold and windy in Chicago, so the game was moved from Wrigley Field to inside Chicago Stadium. The Bears and their opponent, the Portsmouth Spartans, were tied at zero in the fourth quarter. But then Chicago scored on a controversial play when quarterback Dutch Brumbaugh handed off to Nagurski, who threw a short pass to Grange in the end zone. League rules at the time mandated that any forward pass be launched from a minimum of five yards behind the line of scrimmage, and the Spartans argued that Grange was not far enough behind the line when he passed. But the score stood, and the Bears won, 9–0.

A year later, 26,000 fans showed up at Wrigley Field to watch the Bears take on the New York Giants for the 1933 NFL championship. Nagurski's passing prowess produced two touchdowns, and the Bears led late in the game, 23–21, when Grange—playing as a defensive back—made a game-saving tackle to preserve Chicago's second straight championship.

By the end of the 1930s, age and injuries had caught up with The Galloping Ghost and Nagurski. Luckily, Halas found a new player who would keep Chicago flying high. That player was Sid Luckman, a talented college running back who was turned into a quarterback after joining the Bears in 1939. With Luckman and center Clyde Turner leading the offense, and lightning-fast safety George McAfee (who was also a star runner and kick returner) sparking the defense, the Bears— nicknamed "The Monsters of the Midway"—went a stunning 37–5–1 from 1940 to 1943.

The Bears played some outstanding games during that stretch, but no performance came as close to perfection as the 1940 NFL Championship Game against the Washington Redskins. Chicago had lost to the Redskins, 7–3, weeks earlier,

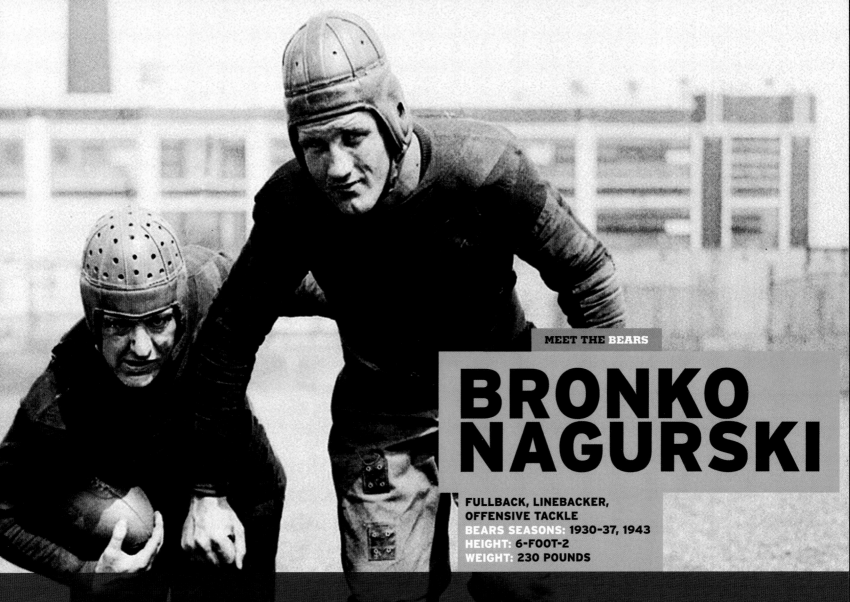

BRONKO NAGURSKI

FULLBACK, LINEBACKER, OFFENSIVE TACKLE
BEARS SEASONS: 1930-37, 1943
HEIGHT: 6-FOOT-2
WEIGHT: 230 POUNDS

Bronko Nagurski was the most powerful football player in America before World War II. Born in Canada and raised in International Falls, Minnesota, Nagurski came from Polish stock. He played collegiate football at the University of Minnesota and had a sensational career there, earning All-American honors on both offense and defense. The Bears signed him in 1930 and soon reaped the benefits of his skill at running, tackling, blocking, and even passing. Often, Nagurski was simply a wrecking ball swinging straight through opposing players. Famed fullback Ernie Nevers of the Duluth Eskimos and Chicago Cardinals once said, "Tackling Bronko was like trying to stop a freight train running downhill." Nagurski helped the Bears win league championships in 1932 and 1933 and then came out of a five-year retirement to help Chicago to another title in 1943 as the Bears defeated the Washington Redskins 41–21. After his football days ended, Nagurski launched a successful career in professional wrestling. Later in life, he retired to International Falls and opened a service station, living to the age of 81.

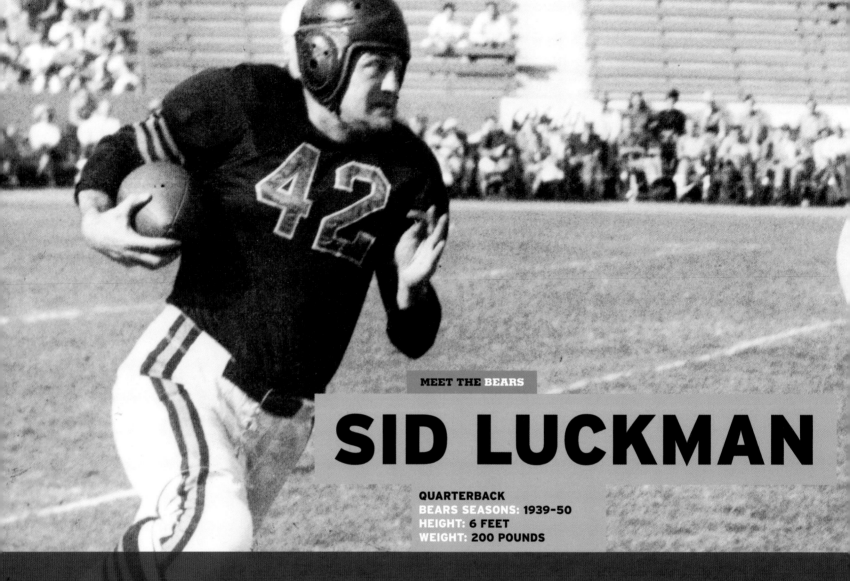

SID LUCKMAN

**QUARTERBACK
BEARS SEASONS: 1939-50
HEIGHT: 6 FEET
WEIGHT: 200 POUNDS**

From 1940 to 1946, the Chicago Bears played in five NFL Championship Games, winning four, and Sid Luckman, the Bears' quarterback and triggerman on their vaunted T-formation attack, was a major reason why. In 1937 and 1938, the Brooklyn-born Luckman was named an All-American at Columbia University. He planned on leaving football behind after college, but legendary Bears coach George Halas gave Luckman a playbook featuring plays from the T-formation, and the idea intrigued Luckman enough that he signed with the Bears in 1939. In 1940, he had a breakout year as the Bears' offense clicked and Chicago stormed to a 73–0 win in the NFL Championship Game versus the Washington Redskins. Equally adept at passing and running, Luckman was also a natural leader. After retiring as a player, he spent many years coaching, including at his alma mater, Columbia University. The school tried to pay Luckman for his efforts, but Luckman refused to accept payment, returning the money with a note that said he'd rather see the money go to a "worthy student."

and when the Bears complained about a controversial call, Redskins owner George Marshall called them "quitters and a bunch of crybabies." In the title game, playing with pride and anger, Chicago destroyed Washington 73–0 in the most lopsided NFL game of all time. It got so bad that the referees eventually asked the Bears to stop kicking extra points. So many balls had been booted into the stands that the officials were running out of footballs. After the game, Redskins quarterback Sammy Baugh was asked if things would have been different if his receiver hadn't dropped a sure touchdown pass that Baugh had thrown in the first quarter. "Sure," said Baugh. "The final score would've been 73–7."

Widely considered the NFL's best center during the 1940s, Clyde Turner (number 66) was also an outstanding linebacker; in 1942, he led the league with 8 interceptions. **X**

YEARS OF THE LEGENDS

x--

The Bears remained a powerful team throughout the 1940s. In 1941, they beat the New York Giants for the NFL championship. In 1942, the Bears were undefeated until the Championship Game, where the Washington Redskins upset them, 14–6. In 1943, however, the Bears got their revenge, besting Washington in a championship rematch, 41–21.

In 1946, after a couple of subpar seasons, Chicago again knocked off the Giants for the NFL championship. But after Luckman retired in 1951, Chicago no longer dominated. As always, the team had a number of terrific players. Running back Rick Casares excited fans with his Nagurski-like rushing style; Harlon Hill became the first Bears player to post more than 1,000 receiving yards in a season; and few players were tougher or more ill-tempered than linebacker Bill George and defensive end Ed Sprinkle. Although Chicago had some moderate success from 1947 to 1962, it made the NFL title game just once, getting routed in 1956 by the Giants, 47–7.

A sense of normalcy finally returned to the Windy City in 1963. That year, behind a tough defense led by 6-foot-8 end Doug Atkins, the Bears went 11–1–2 and took on the Giants for the championship. The Giants had a great offense that featured running back Frank Gifford and quarterback Y. A. Tittle, but the Bears featured a physical

X Linebacker Bill George (left) excelled through aggression and craftiness, while defensive end Doug Atkins (right) was regarded by many as the strongest man in football.

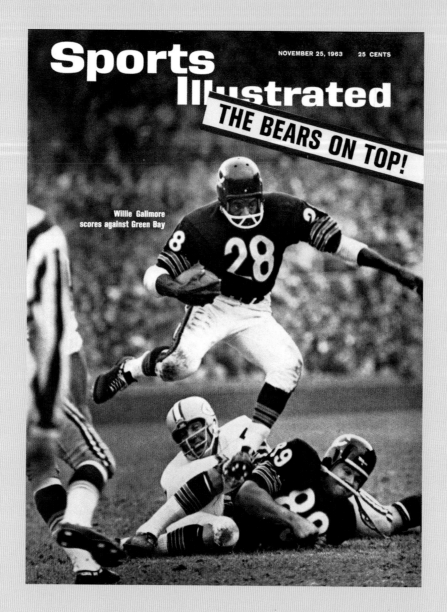

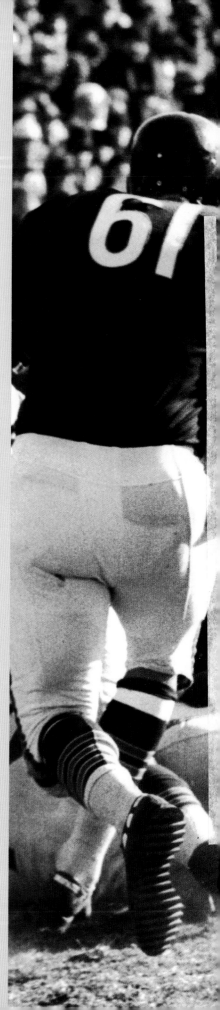

defense that had surrendered an average of just 10 points per game during the season. True to form, the Chicago defense allowed the Giants just 10 points as it intercepted 5 passes and knocked Tittle around so much that he needed pain-numbing injections on the sideline just to keep going. Chicago put up 14 points of its own with 2 touchdown-scoring quarterback sneaks by Billy Wade to capture its eighth world championship.

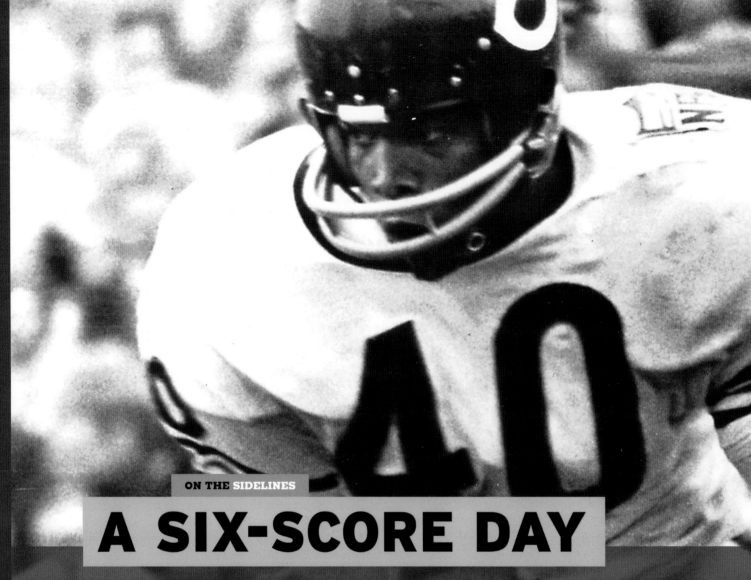

ON THE SIDELINES

A SIX-SCORE DAY

December 12, 1965, was a cold and wet day in Chicago. The Chicago Bears and San Francisco 49ers were suited up to play, and after players tested the field in pre-game warm-ups, most readied themselves for what they presumed would be a grind-it-out game on the sloppy Wrigley Field turf. But on the second play of the game, Gale Sayers, a rookie Bears running back nicknamed "The Kansas Comet," caught a short screen pass and darted through the entire 49ers defense for a touchdown. In the second quarter, Sayers took a pitch-out 21 yards for a score, and then followed that up with a 7-yard jaunt to pay dirt. And that was just the first half. In the second half, Sayers scored three more touchdowns for an NFL record of six in one game. The final score came by way of an electrifying 85-yard punt return. Sayers's performance left all those in attendance amazed. "The mud affected the kid," said Bears tight end Mike Ditka after the game. "If it had been dry out there, he would've scored 10 touchdowns."

Bears fans didn't know it yet, but 1963 would be the last hurrah for a while in Chicago. Over the next 20 years, the Bears would put together just 4 winning seasons. The NFL was expanding to include more teams, and talent became more thinly spread throughout the league. Still, the Bears of the early 1960s were exciting to watch. They had two stars in Atkins and Mike Ditka—a hard-as-nails end who was both a sure-handed receiver and a devastating blocker—and in the 1965 NFL Draft, they added two more: running back Gale Sayers and linebacker Dick Butkus.

Equally spectacular as a rusher, receiver, and kick returner, Sayers was lightning on cleats. Fans and teammates would watch in amazement as he hurdled defenders and zigzagged clear across the field with his long stride. In one game against the San Francisco 49ers during his rookie season, Sayers scored an NFL-record six touchdowns—one on a pass, four on runs, and one on an 85-yard punt return. Sadly, his career spanned only parts of seven seasons before being cut short by knee injuries.

While Sayers bewildered opponents, Butkus frightened them. Regarded by many as the most ferocious football player of all time, the 6-foot-3 and 245-pound linebacker played every snap with reckless abandon. Even though the

X Even though Gale Sayers played just five full NFL seasons, the Hall of Fame welcomed him in 1977, noting, "There was never another to compare with him."

X The fury with which Dick Butkus played earned him various nicknames, including "The Animal" and "The Maestro of Mayhem."

Bears had a winning record only twice during his nine-year career, Butkus never stopped giving his all. "It's like he was from another world, another planet," Miami Dolphins guard Bob Kuechenberg later marveled. "He didn't run a [fast 40-yard dash], he wasn't a great weight lifter, but he just ate them alive, all those ... sprinters and 500-pound bench pressers."

BRIAN'S SONG

Brian Piccolo joined the Bears in 1966, one year after Gale Sayers, and the two shared not only a common position at running back but also a similar zest for life. Unfortunately, late in the 1969 season, a large cancerous tumor was found in Piccolo's left lung. During Piccolo's struggles with cancer and recuperations from surgeries, Sayers had knee surgery, which required long bouts of rehabilitation. The two players encouraged each other through their respective hardships. While Sayers eventually recovered, Piccolo did not and died on June 16, 1970, at age 26. Sayers was so moved by Piccolo's courage that he wrote a memoir largely about his friendship with Piccolo, which became the basis for a made-for-television movie called *Brian's Song*. In addition to being a poignant story about friendship, life, death, and football, the movie had an unexpected effect on viewers. While America wrestled with race riots and race discrimination, the movie, about a black man and a white man befriending and helping one another, offered an intelligent look at the fulfillment that could come from such helpful and unprejudiced friendships.

[27]

DICK BUTKUS

LINEBACKER
BEARS SEASONS: 1965-73
HEIGHT: 6-FOOT-3
WEIGHT: 245 POUNDS

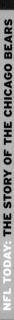

With a mean streak a mile wide and the ability to intimidate even the toughest ballcarriers, Dick Butkus cut an imposing figure on the football field for the Bears. Butkus grew up on the south side of Chicago and was a two-time All-American at the University of Illinois. He joined the Bears in 1965 along with another impressive Bears rookie, running back Gale Sayers. Playing a tough sport, manning a tough position, often wearing a tough-looking mustache, and even having a tough-sounding name, Butkus quickly became a fan favorite. "When I went out on the field to warm up, I would manufacture things to make me mad," he once said to explain his on-field fierceness. "If someone on the other team was laughing, I'd pretend he was laughing at me or the Bears. It always worked for me." After a serious knee injury cut his stellar playing career short, he went on to some success as a television and commercial actor and announcer. As a tribute to his legendary defensive skills, the Dick Butkus Award is handed out yearly to college football's top linebacker.

When Butkus retired after the 1973 season, fans had to wait just one year for the next Bears legend to emerge. That player was Walter Payton, a running back who, as a kid, had been more interested in band and gymnastics than football. Although Payton weighed just 200 pounds and was nicknamed "Sweetness," he was a classic Bears rusher who enjoyed running over—not around—defenders. Amazingly, despite his hard-nosed running style, he would miss only 1 game in his 13-year career.

From 1976 to 1986, Payton rushed for more than 1,000 yards every season but one (only a players' strike in 1982 broke the streak). Before his playing days ended, Sweetness would carry the ball more times (3,838) for more yards (16,726) than any player in NFL history. Perhaps the most remarkable thing was that he did it despite the mediocre talent in Chicago during most of those years. As former San Diego Chargers tight end Kellen Winslow noted, "For most of his career, he took on the NFL with no offensive line."

BEARS THRIVE IN '85

In 1982, 87-year-old George Halas, who still owned the team, put the Bears in the hands of a new coach: former star end Mike Ditka. "Iron Mike" had earned a reputation as a tough guy during his playing days in the 1960s, and the fiery coach soon had the team on the rise. Behind the great play of Payton, young quarterback Jim McMahon, safety Gary Fencik, defensive end Dan Hampton, and linebacker Mike Singletary, the Bears went 8–8 in 1983 and 10–6 in 1984.

By 1985, the Bears were poised for greatness. Payton was still explosive, and Chicago's defense—molded by feisty defensive coordinator Buddy Ryan—was the NFL's best. The Bears won their first 12 games in 1985 and finished with a 15–1 record. Defensive end Richard Dent led the NFL with 17 quarterback sacks, and the hard-hitting Singletary was named the league's Defensive Player of the Year.

In the playoffs, the Bears were unstoppable. They crushed the New York Giants 21–0 and the Los Angeles Rams 24–0 to reach the Super Bowl. They then destroyed the New England Patriots 46–10 to capture the franchise's ninth world championship. "We've been working hard the last two years to be the best [defense] ever," said Dent after the victory. "I believe we're in the running. If we're not, I'd like to see who's better."

X End Richard Dent (number 95) was a star among stars on the 1985 Bears defense; in Super Bowl XX, he notched two sacks, forced two fumbles, and batted down a Patriots pass.

X Halfback Neal Anderson (pictured) did his best to fill Walter Payton's shoes, galloping for more than 1,000 yards in 1988, 1989, and 1990.

Chicago continued to dominate the National Football Conference (NFC) Central Division in the seasons that followed. Between 1984 and 1988, the Bears won 62 games—then the most ever by any NFL team in a five-year span. They remained a league power through 1991 with the help of such additions as running back Neal Anderson (who replaced the retired Payton). Unfortunately, the Bears could not make it back to the Super Bowl. In 1992, after Chicago went just 5–11, Ditka stepped down as head coach.

X Although often controversial in his behavior off the field, Jim McMahon was a confident general on the field, showing rare poise under pressure.

With Ditka and most of the stars of the 1980s gone, Chicago was a mediocre team for the rest of the '90s. Dave Wannstedt was hired as Chicago's new head coach in 1993, and Bears fans shared brief optimism when the team went 9–7 in 1994 and won an opening-round playoff game against the Minnesota Vikings before bowing out to the eventual-champion San Francisco 49ers in the next round. But the Bears would not make the playoffs again in Wannstedt's tenure, which lasted through the 1998 season. Bad luck abounded during those years, as several promising young players—including running back Rashaan Salaam and quarterback Cade McNown—had short careers due to injuries or disappointing play after the Bears spent high draft picks to acquire them.

In 2000, with head coach Dick Jauron at the helm, the Bears finally added the star they so desperately needed: linebacker Brian Urlacher. At 6-foot-4 and 260 pounds, Urlacher's size and skill (not to mention his crew-cut hairstyle) had people comparing him to the great Butkus. In his first NFL season, Urlacher lived up to the hype by making 165 tackles and earning Defensive Rookie of the Year honors. "It seems like he gets to places faster than anyone else," marveled Bears safety Mike Brown, also a

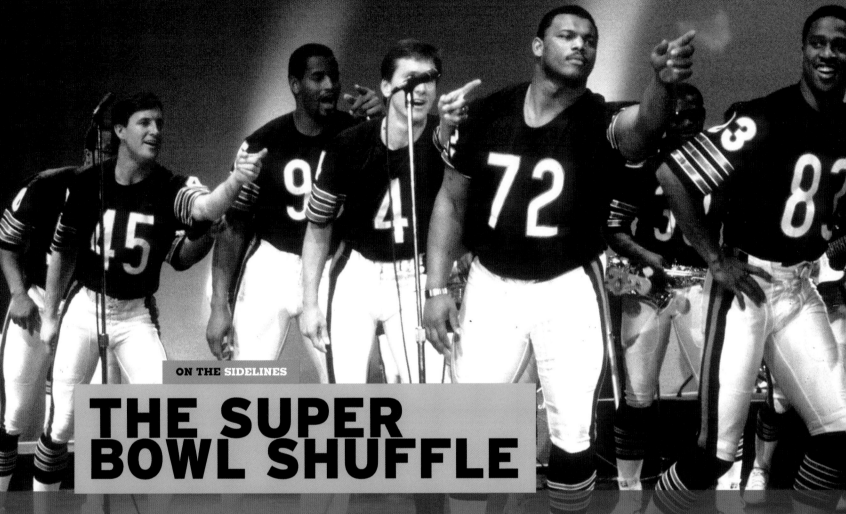

THE SUPER BOWL SHUFFLE

Although the 1985 Chicago Bears weren't the first NFL team to sing and dance to a rally song, "The Super Bowl Shuffle" is probably the best-remembered and most widely known such song. Before the Bears' appearance in Super Bowl XX, numerous members of the team, including running back Walter Payton, quarterback Jim McMahon, linebacker Mike Singletary, receiver Willie Gault, defensive end Richard Dent, and defensive lineman William "The Refrigerator" Perry, got together to sing and dance to a rap song that was the brainchild of Gault and record producer Randy Weigand. Players took turns rapping and singing the chorus, "We ain't here to start no trouble, we're just here to do the Super Bowl Shuffle." The song and resulting music video were smash hits when they reached airwaves and television. "The Super Bowl Shuffle" reached #41 on the Billboard Charts and #75 on the Hot R&B/Hip-Hop Chart. It was also nominated for a Grammy award in the Best Rhythm and Blues Vocal Performance category. Some profits for the song went to charity, quelling some of the criticism the team received for being "cocky."

MIKE DITKA

TIGHT END, COACH
BEARS SEASONS: 1961-66
(AS PLAYER), 1982-92 (AS COACH)
HEIGHT: 6-FOOT-3
WEIGHT: 230 POUNDS

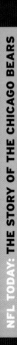

As both a player and a coach in the NFL, Mike Ditka was a success. Selected by the Bears with the fifth overall pick in the 1961 NFL Draft, Ditka went on to enjoy an extraordinary rookie season in which he caught 56 passes for 1,076 yards and 12 touchdowns and won league Rookie of the Year honors. Players such as Ditka, who had the sheer size to throw crushing blocks and the agility and sure hands to catch passes, helped increase the value teams placed on the tight end position. After his playing career, he turned to coaching, and the tenacity and ferocity that Ditka possessed as a player served him well on the sidelines. Some fans consider the 1985 Bears team that won Super Bowl XX under Coach Ditka to be the best team of all time. As both a player and coach, Ditka knew how to win. "There's more to winning than just wanting to," he once said. "You have to prove yourself every Sunday. Just throwing your helmet on the field doesn't scare anyone."

rookie in 2000. "I've never seen someone so fast on the football field."

In 2001, the Bears ended their streak of losing football by putting together a surprising 13–3 record. Led by an aggressive defense headed by Urlacher and Brown, the Bears kept fans on the edges of their seats week after week, winning a number of games with frantic comebacks and trick plays. In back-to-back midseason games, the scrappy Bears came back late from 15 points down to the 49ers and 14 points down to the Cleveland Browns to win both games in overtime on interception returns by Brown. After getting a bye in the first round of the playoffs, the Bears drew the Philadelphia Eagles in the second round and briefly led 7–6 before the Eagles took control and won, 33–19.

X A hard hitter who seemed to play bigger than his 5-foot-10 frame, safety Mike Brown (number 30) earned All-Pro honors in 2001.

ALL YOU NEED IS LOVIE

The next two seasons were rife with injury and underachievement as Chicago went 4–12 and then 7–9. Jauron was relieved of his coaching duties, and former St. Louis Rams defensive coordinator Lovie Smith was signed on. Right away, Smith pointed to three clear goals he wanted to attain as Chicago's new coach: end the decade of dominance that the rival Green Bay Packers had held over the Bears, control the newly formed NFC North Division, and win the Super Bowl.

Smith had grown up in Big Sandy, Texas, and was a part of one of the most dominant high school football teams in modern history. In 1975, Big Sandy outscored its opponents 824–15 on its way to its third straight state championship. Smith had a stellar playing career as a linebacker and safety at the University of Tulsa and then headed straight into coaching. He spent time as an assistant coach at many colleges and in the NFL before landing the Bears job.

Smith's first season in Chicago, 2004, was far from exceptional, as the Bears lost their starting quarterback,

Rex Grossman, to a season-ending injury in the third game and shuffled through three other quarterbacks the rest of the year en route to a 5–11 mark. Still, the defense was fast improving, thanks to players such as Urlacher, cornerback Nathan Vasher, and defensive tackle Tommie Harris.

The 2005 Bears got it together for their new coach, going 11–5. Although Grossman again was lost to injury for the majority of the season, the Bears' defense was one of the best in the league, with five members heading to the Pro Bowl after the season. Although Chicago lost its first-round playoff game 29–21 to the Carolina Panthers, Coach Smith was universally praised for turning the Bears around, garnering NFL Coach of the Year honors.

With Grossman finally healthy and running back Thomas Jones coming off a 1,335-yard rushing season, the 2006 Bears offense finally began operating at full speed and giving Chicago a more balanced attack. Adding to the team's offensive firepower was rookie return man Devin Hester, who ran three punts and two kickoffs back for touchdowns using his uncanny ability to weave through the sea of players speeding at him on special teams. The Bears finished the regular season an NFC-best 13–3 and earned home-field advantage throughout the playoffs.

FRIDGE'S SUPER SCORE

Never much of a quarterback sacker, 6-foot-2 and 350-pound defensive tackle William "The Refrigerator" Perry instead plugged holes in the line and stuffed running backs for nearly nine seasons with the Chicago Bears. In 1985, he was a precocious rookie who happened to fit into coach Mike Ditka's plans—occasionally on offense as well as defense. In goal-line offensive situations, Ditka would bring in Perry and place him in the backfield. From that spot, Perry could throw massive blocks, take the handoff in for the score (as he did twice during the regular season), or even catch the ball (which he did once) for a touchdown. With the Bears thumping the New England Patriots 37–3 in Super Bowl XX and Chicago on the goal line yet again, Ditka called on The Fridge. Perry was given the ball and rolled out as if to pass, but he was tackled for a one-yard loss. Unfazed, the Bears handed off to him again, and this time, The Fridge stomped into the end zone for his Super Bowl touchdown.

ON THE SIDELINES

PRIME-TIME RETURN MAN

Super Bowl XLI, after the 2006 season, pitted the Bears against the Indianapolis Colts. With the rock song "Welcome to the Jungle" wafting through the stadium's speakers, the opening kickoff by the Colts was suddenly in the air, and as rookie Chicago kick returner Devin Hester settled under it at the eight-yard line, many fans had yet to settle in their seats. The Bears' number 23 caught the ball near the left sideline and immediately veered right, heading up the field. He hesitated for just an instant, faking left before continuing to the right, then put on a blazing burst of speed to get around the Colts' coverage team. Seconds later, Hester coasted into the end zone, thus becoming the first player in Super Bowl history to return the opening kickoff for a touchdown. "That gave us a big lift right away," said Chicago coach Lovie Smith. "Whenever you can start a game off like that, it gives you a lot of momentum." Although the momentum wouldn't last—the Bears ultimately lost the game by a 29–17 score—Hester's return was a moment Chicago fans would never forget.

First up were the Seattle Seahawks, against whom the Bears pulled out a 27–24 win on a field goal in overtime. Then, a week later, Chicago secured a place in the Super Bowl with a 39–14 trouncing of the New Orleans Saints. Super Bowl XLI, played in Miami, featured the strong passing attack of the Indianapolis Colts, led by quarterback Peyton Manning, versus the tough Bears defense. Hester immediately sparked Chicago when he took the game's opening kickoff 92 yards for a touchdown. Manning steadied the Colts, though, and despite a late Chicago comeback, Indianapolis pulled out the victory, 29–17. "We just never really established any kind of rhythm, running or throwing it, until it was too late," Grossman said.

X Although he was a patient and soft-spoken leader, coach Lovie Smith preached a physically punishing brand of football, especially on defense.

Few NFL teams swarmed to the ball as effectively as the Bears; in both 2001 and 2005, Chicago boasted the league's top-ranked defense.

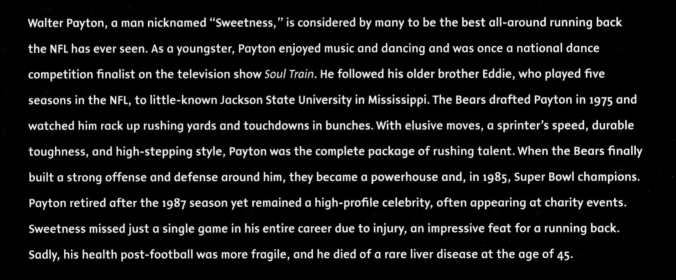

WALTER PAYTON

RUNNING BACK
BEARS SEASONS: 1975-87
HEIGHT: 5-FOOT-10
WEIGHT: 200 POUNDS

Walter Payton, a man nicknamed "Sweetness," is considered by many to be the best all-around running back

the NFL has ever seen. As a youngster, Payton enjoyed music and dancing and was once a national dance

competition finalist on the television show *Soul Train*. He followed his older brother Eddie, who played five

seasons in the NFL, to little-known Jackson State University in Mississippi. The Bears drafted Payton in 1975 and

watched him rack up rushing yards and touchdowns in bunches. With elusive moves, a sprinter's speed, durable

toughness, and high-stepping style, Payton was the complete package of rushing talent. When the Bears finally

built a strong offense and defense around him, they became a powerhouse and, in 1985, Super Bowl champions.

Payton retired after the 1987 season yet remained a high-profile celebrity, often appearing at charity events.

Sweetness missed just a single game in his entire career due to injury, an impressive feat for a running back.

Sadly, his health post-football was more fragile, and he died of a rare liver disease at the age of 45.

Chicago's 2007 campaign was marred by a slew of injuries, bad play, and missed opportunities that resulted in a 7–9 record. Hester was one of the few highlights, setting an NFL record with six punt or kickoff returns for touchdowns and forcing many teams to kick the ball away from him. To avoid "The Windy City Flyer," one coach, Rod Marinelli of the Detroit Lions, told his punter to "kick the ball into Lake Michigan and make sure it sinks to the bottom."

In 2008, the Bears re-signed Tommie Harris to anchor the defense along with Urlacher and fellow linebacker Lance Briggs. Although many experts had low expectations for Chicago heading into the 2008 season, the Bears once again defied expectations, staying in the NFC North hunt with a 9–7 record thanks to the efforts of the always tough defense and surprisingly strong play by quarterback Kyle Orton and rookie running back Matt Forte.

Since their start in Chicago in 1921, the Bears have put together one of the richest and most decorated histories in the NFL. By 2008, Chicago had produced dozens of Hall-of-Famers, won nine league championships, and earned the support of Bears fans worldwide. Today, fresh off the franchise's second Super Bowl berth, a new generation of Bears are looking to become Monsters of the Midway once again.

INDEX